THE NATURE KIDS GUIDE TO

RED PANDAS

DAVID ANDERSON

LP Media Inc. Publishing
Text copyright © 2026 by LP Media Inc.

For information address LP Media Inc. Publishing,
30012 Variolite St NW, Princeton MN 55371
www.lpmedia.org

Publication Data

Red Pandas
The Nature Kid's Guide to Red Pandas — First edition.

Summary: "Learn all about Red Pandas, the Nature Kid Way"
— Provided by publisher.

ISBN: 979-8-89818-112-3

[1. Red Pandas - Non-Fiction] I. Title.

Title: The Nature Kid's Guide to Red Pandas

CONTENTS

MISTY MOUNTAINS

Rustle! A red panda moves through foggy trees. It looks for bamboo.

Red pandas live in cool mountain forests. Thick clouds and mist often cover the tall trees. The air stays damp and chilly all year long.

Bamboo grows everywhere in these misty woods. Soft green moss covers the tree bark. Ferns and bushes fill the forest floor. Water drips from leaves in the foggy air.

Red pandas need this cool, wet home to survive. It is the perfect **habitat** for them. The trees give them places to sleep and hide. Their thick fur keeps them warm but makes hot weather hard. They feel best in the cool mountain mist.

ASIAN HOMES

Snap! A red panda walks along a branch in Asia. Its fluffy tail sways.

Red pandas live in Asia. You can find them in only five countries. These countries are located in the Himalayan mountain range and the surrounding regions of southwestern China.

Red pandas stay high in the mountains. They live between 6,600 and 14,000 feet up. That is very high! Clouds and fog cover the trees. Red pandas like forests with lots of bamboo. They also need trees to climb and rest in.

Red pandas share their mountain homes with snow leopards but rarely meet them.

CAT SIZED

Crunch! A small, furry red panda sits on a log. It munches on bamboo.

Red pandas are about the size of a house cat. They weigh between 8 and 14 pounds. Their bodies are 20 to 26 inches long.

Their bushy tails add 12 to 20 more inches. This long tail helps them balance in trees. It also keeps them warm when they sleep.

Red pandas have short legs. Their front legs are shorter than their back legs. This helps them climb down trees head first!

Red pandas are much smaller than giant pandas, which can weigh over 200 pounds.

RUSTY RED

DID YOU KNOW?
Red panda fur has two layers. The outer layer is long and coarse for protection.

Yawn! A red panda stretches on a branch. Its rusty fur glows in the sun.

Red pandas have rusty red fur on their backs. This color matches the reddish moss on trees where they live. Their bellies and legs are black, which helps them blend into shadows.

White marks cover their faces. They have white eyebrows and white patches on their cheeks. Each red panda has a different face pattern.

Their tails have red and tan rings. The rings make their tails look striped. Their feet are special too. Thick white fur covers the bottoms of their feet.

SUPER
SNIFFERS

Sniff, sniff! A red panda lifts its nose. It smells the air.

Red pandas have a strong sense of smell. Their noses help them find bamboo hidden in thick forests.

Red pandas also use smell to find other red pandas. They leave scent marks on trees and rocks.

Their whiskers help them explore too. Whiskers sense things nearby, even in the dark.

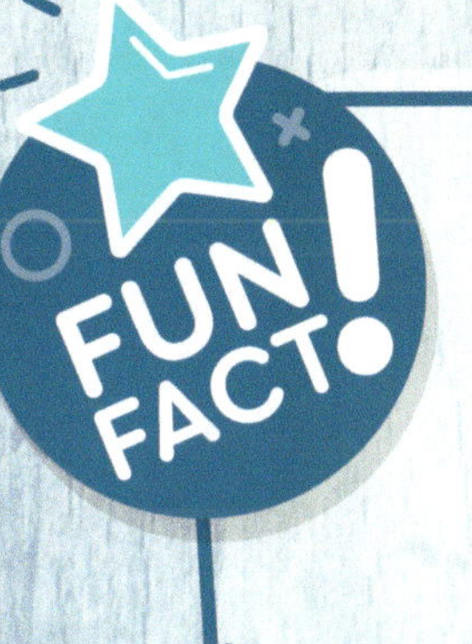

Red pandas have scent glands on the bottoms of their feet. As they walk around, they leave their smell behind on branches and the ground. This tells other red pandas "I live here!"

HIDE WELL

Hiss! A red panda freezes on a mossy branch. It stays very still.

Red pandas hide well in their forest homes. Their rusty red fur blends with reddish-brown moss and bark. Predators have trouble spotting them.

Red pandas curl into tight balls when resting. They cover their faces with their bushy tails. This makes them look like clumps of moss.

They also stay very still when scared. Not moving helps them stay hidden from eagles and snow leopards.

Red pandas can sleep for up to 17 hours a day, hidden high in the trees.

BAMBOO
LUNCH

Chomp! A red panda bites into a crunchy bamboo stem.

Red pandas eat mostly bamboo. They munch on bamboo leaves and young shoots. Bamboo is not very filling, so they eat a lot of it.

They spend many hours eating each day. This helps them get enough **nutrients** from the bamboo.

Red pandas also eat some other foods. They sometimes eat berries, fruits, and bird eggs. They will also snack on insects and small lizards.

Red pandas can eat 20,000 bamboo leaves a day.

CHIRPS AND CHATTER

FUN FACT!

Red pandas can make a sound called a "huff-quack" when they are startled.

Chirp! A red panda calls out from a tree branch.

Red pandas are usually quiet animals. They spend most of their time alone. But they still need ways to talk to each other.

These animals make soft sounds. They chirp and squeak. Baby red pandas whistle when they want their mother. Adults huff when they feel upset.

Red pandas also use smell to send messages. They leave scent marks on trees and rocks.

Body language matters too. A scared red panda stands on its back legs. It raises its front paws up high.

WATCH OUT

DID YOU KNOW?
Baby red pandas face more danger than adults because they cannot climb fast yet.

Screech! A hawk circles above the trees. A red panda hides below.

Red pandas have several predators in the wild. Snow leopards hunt them in the mountains. Martens also chase red pandas through the trees.

Large birds are dangerous too. Hawks and other birds of prey swoop down from the sky. They try to catch young red pandas.

Wild dogs and jackals hunt red pandas on the ground. These fast predators can chase them quickly.

Red pandas must always stay alert to survive.

QUICK
CLIMB

Whoosh! A red panda races up a tall tree trunk. It moves fast!

Red pandas climb trees to escape danger. They scramble up trunks very fast. Their sharp claws dig into bark to help them grip.

Red pandas have flexible ankles. Their back feet can turn almost all the way around. This helps them climb down headfirst.

Once up high, red pandas rest on branches. Predators cannot follow them easily.

TREE
TRICKS

Click! A red panda grips a branch. It hangs upside down to reach leaves.

Red pandas are amazing tree climbers. They spend most of their time in trees.

Red pandas can walk along very thin branches without falling. Their long, bushy tails help them balance. They can also leap from branch to branch with ease.

They can even hang from branches using their back legs. This frees up their front paws to grab food and bring it to their mouths.

Red pandas have flexible ankles that rotate. This helps them climb down trees headfirst.

SLEEPY DAYS

Yawn! A red panda curls up on a branch. It is nap time.

Red pandas sleep a lot during the day. They rest in trees on thick branches.

Red pandas are most active at dawn and dusk. This is when they search for food.

A tree branch makes the perfect bed. Red pandas curl up into a tight ball. Their fluffy tail works like a blanket. It covers their face and keeps them warm.

Red pandas sometimes sleep in different trees each day, moving to new spots to stay safe from predators.

SOLO STARS

Stomp! A red panda walks alone through the forest.

Red pandas almost always live alone. Each one has its own space in the forest.

Living alone means they do not have to share food. Bamboo does not give them much energy. So they need a lot of it for themselves.

Red pandas mark their area with scent. They rub glands on trees and rocks. This tells other red pandas to stay away.

Males and females only meet to have babies.

Red pandas taste scents with their tongues. This helps them find food and other red pandas.

WINTER WHISTLES

Chirp! A red panda calls out in the cold winter air.

Red pandas mate in winter. This is from January to March. Males and females find each other in the cold.

Males make soft sounds. They chirp and whistle. They call through the trees. Females listen for these calls.

After mating, the male leaves. The female raises the babies alone. Cubs are born about four months later. They come in early summer.

Males travel long distances through the forest to find females during mating season.

CUTE CUBS

DID YOU KNOW?
Red panda mothers have one to four cubs at a time. Newborn cubs weigh only about four ounces.

Squeak! A tiny red panda cub peeks out from a nest.

Red panda cubs are born in summer. They are very small at birth, weighing about as much as a stick of butter.

Cubs are born with their eyes closed. They cannot see for about three weeks. Their fur is gray at first, but it turns red as they grow older.

Cubs stay in the nest for around three months. During this time, they drink milk from their mother. By fall, they start to eat bamboo leaves.

MOM KNOWS
DID YOU KNOW?
Mothers lick cubs clean to keep the den smell-free from predators.

Growl! A mother red panda guards her den. She keeps her babies safe inside.

Mother red pandas do all the parenting. They raise their cubs without help from fathers, and they are very protective.

Before giving birth, mothers build cozy nests. They use grass, leaves, and twigs to line hollow trees or rock cracks.

Mothers carry cubs in their mouths to move them. This helps them find a new hiding spot if danger is near. Cubs stay with their mothers for about one year. During this time, mothers teach their cubs how to climb and find food. The cubs watch and copy what their mother does.

FORESTS FALLING

Crack! A tree falls in the forest. A red panda watches its home disappear.

Red pandas are in danger. People cut down forests where they live. This destroys their homes and food.

Farmers clear land to grow crops. They also let cows and goats eat forest plants. This leaves less bamboo for red pandas.

Roads split forests into small pieces. Red pandas need connected forests to survive.

Fewer than 10,000 red pandas live in the wild. They have lost half their forest homes in just 20 years.

HELPING HANDS

Thump! A red panda lands safely in a zoo habitat. Help is here.

Many people work to save red pandas. Zoos help keep them safe. Zoos raise baby red pandas. They teach people about them too. When people learn about them, they want to help.

Scientists study red pandas in the wild. They watch where they go. They see what they eat.

Some groups plant new bamboo forests. They also work to stop people from cutting down trees.

Over 80 zoos work together to help red pandas survive and grow their numbers.

GLOSSARY

body language
the way an animal moves its body to show how it feels

scent glands
body parts that make a special smell an animal uses to leave messages for other animals

habitat
The place where an animal lives in nature

mating season
The time of year when animals find partners to have babies.

nutrients
Good things in food that help bodies grow and stay healthy.